Contents

Biff, Chip and Kipper have lost some objects from their magic key adventures. Can you find them in this book?

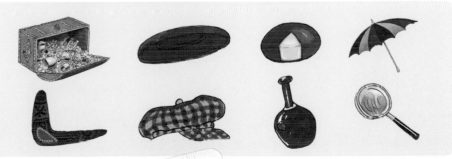

Meet the children

Biff

Birthday:	20 May
Likes:	making things
Dislikes:	wearing dresses
Favourite animal:	koala
Favourite word:	chopsticks
Favourite magic key adventure (...so far!):	Wilf and I helped stop thieves from stealing a blue jewel.

Chip

Birthday:	20 May
Likes:	art
Dislikes:	quarrelling
Favourite animal:	dolphin
Favourite word:	volcano
Favourite magic key adventure (...so far!):	My plan caught the evil genie and saved Floppy.

Kipper

Birthday:	7 April
Likes:	reading
Dislikes:	tidying up
Favourite animal:	Floppy
Favourite word:	bubble
Favourite magic key adventure (...so far!):	I tricked the Sheriff's men to save everyone.

Wilf

Birthday:	8 July
Likes:	cycling
Dislikes:	people who won't share
Favourite animal:	tree frog
Favourite word:	dinosaur
Favourite magic key adventure (...so far!):	I used my chewing gum to hide some gold.

Wilma

Birthday: 31 October
Likes: music
Dislikes: mess
Favourite animal: polar bear
Favourite word: harmony
Favourite magic key adventure (...so far!): I went on a quest to rescue a crystal bell.

Anneena

Birthday: 6 February
Likes: making up games
Dislikes: swimming
Favourite animal: garter snake
Favourite word: velvet
Favourite magic key adventure (...so far!): Nadim and I helped some men to try and make their aeroplane fly.

Nadim

Birthday: 13 January
Likes: computers
Dislikes: singing
Favourite animal: panda
Favourite word: rainbow
Favourite magic key adventure (...so far!): It was exciting when my computer game came to life.

Lee

Birthday: / June
Likes: gadgets
Dislikes: scary stories
Favourite animal: rabbit
Favourite word: monster
Favourite magic key adventure (...so far!): I met some ogres. I was a bit scared at first.

Spot the difference

The Robinson family have moved house. Can you find the house they live in now?

There are 10 differences between the two pictures. Can you find them all?

The answers can be found on page 32.

5

The secret room

Biff and Chip helped to pull the wallpaper off.

Biff and Chip liked the new house. Biff wanted new wallpaper in her room. Mum and Dad pulled the old wallpaper off.

Biff found a door. The door was stuck.

Mum opened the door. She found a room. Everyone looked inside.

Mum went into the secret room. She found a little house.

It looks like our house.

Biff opened the little house. Everyone looked inside.

It looks like our house inside.

Kipper found a little dog.

It looks like our dog. It looks like Floppy.

Chip found three little children.

They look like us.

Biff liked her bedroom and the secret room.

Biff dreamed about the little children.

Now read *The Secret Room* (Level 4 Stories).

How to draw Floppy

Would you like to draw Floppy? Alex Brychta shows you how to do it.

You will need:
A pencil or pen
A piece of paper

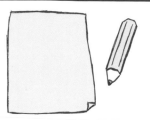

1.

Start by drawing Floppy's nose.

2.

Above his nose, add his eyes and the top of his head.

3.

Then add his ears.

4.

Draw his mouth.

5.

Then add his collar.

6.

Draw his front legs.

7.

Add his back legs. One on each side!

8.

Don't forget his tail!

You have a drawing of Floppy!

Now all you need to do is colour me in!

Save Floppy!

Biff and Chip need to rescue Floppy. Can you help them to find a way to Floppy? Make sure you don't meet the evil genie on the way!

Start ▶

Finish

The storm

There was a storm. The wind blew. The rain came down.

Oh no!

What a mess!

The tree was down.

Floppy found something.
It was a box.

Everyone looked at the box. Mum opened it.

They found
a key inside.

Chip wanted the
box. He put it
in his room.

Now read *The Storm* (Level 4 Stories).

Where are Biff, Chip and Kipper?

Biff, Chip, Kipper and Floppy have been taken on an adventure. Can you find them? Can you find the magic key to get them home again?

What else can you see? Can you spot these things:

- A bear
- Robin Hood
- A monster
- A pair of knights playing football
- A dragon toasting marshmallows
- A knight with his helmet on backwards
- 5 of Floppy's bones
- 4 pairs of glasses

How the magic key works

Chip, Kipper and I found a magic key. It takes us on exciting adventures to lots of different places. Do you know how we get there? Let me tell you.

First, the key glows. We never know when it will glow or where it will take us.

We zoom towards the door of the little house and we start to shrink.

We are carried into the little house in something called a vortex.

The laughing princess

Try and make me laugh.

Chip had a book about a princess who couldn't laugh.

The magic key took them on a new adventure.

PERSON WANTED TO MAKE THE PRINCESS LAUGH REWARD

People were lining up to try and make the princess laugh.

The king was in the village.

That's not funny.

Kipper had a go.

That will make the princess laugh.

18

Kipper dropped the teeth. A dog took them. Everyone ran.

Stop that dog!

Get the teeth!

Oh no!

Now they won't make the princess laugh.

The magic key began to glow. It was time to go home.

The princess saw the king. She laughed.

Now read *The Laughing Princess* (Level 6 More Stories A).

The great race

Join Gran, Biff and Chip in the great race!

1

2

You will need:

A counter for each player
A dice

How to play:

- Take it in turns. Pick a player to start.
- Roll the dice. Move the counter the number of squares shown on the dice. If you land on a square with instructions on it, follow what they say.
- The first player to get to the finish is the winner.

13 The Baron says, "Ha. You won't win." Go back 4.

14

15

16

17

18

19

33

32

31

30 The Baron puts oil on the road. Roll a 2 to carry on.

29

The car skids on the oil! Gran is in front! Go forward to 35.

34

35

36 The bridge is dangerous. Miss a go.

3

4 Gran chooses her car. Go forward 2.

5

6

7

8

12

11

10 Biff, Chip and Gran look at the map. Go forward 1.

9

RACE THIS WAY

20

21 A man changes the signpost. Go back 2.

22

23 The map blows away. Miss a go.

24

28

27

26 Gran doesn't see the signpost. She goes the right way. Go forward 2.

25

37

38 The Baron's car crashes into the river. Go forward to 39.

39

40 Finish

Now read *The Great Race* (Level 5 More Stories A).

Meeting the Romans

Biff and Chip did a project on the Romans at school. They learned about:

Roman chariots ...

... and chariot racing.

Roman leaders, called Emperors.

Roman buildings and the city of Rome.

Can you find out anything else about ancient Rome?

The magic key took Biff and Chip to ancient Rome. They helped a family make pizza for the Emperor. Make your own pizza.

Dad tried to help!

Ingredients (makes 2):

- 2 pitta breads to use as pizza bases – or you can use a small baguette sliced in half
- 2 tablespoons tomato puree
- 8 cherry tomatoes
- Toppings that you like – mushrooms, peppers, tinned sweetcorn, onion, tomatoes, courgettes, olives
- 50g grated cheese – you could use mozzarella or cheddar

Equipment:

- An adult to help you
- Measuring scales
- A tablespoon
- Bowl
- A knife (for adult use)
- A cheese grater
- An oven preheated to 200°C (for adult use)
- A baking tray

You can also use gluten-free bread and non-dairy cheese.

What to do:

1. Before cooking, wash your hands.
2. Chop the cherry tomatoes and put them in a bowl. Add the tomato puree and mix together.
3. Spoon the tomato mixture on to your pizza bases and spread it out.
4. Ask an adult to help you to chop your toppings and add them to your pizzas.
5. Sprinkle the cheese over the top of your pizzas.
6. Ask an adult to put the pizzas on a baking tray and put them in the oven for 10 minutes.
7. Eat your pizza – be careful, it will be hot!

Now read *Roman Adventure* (Level 8 More Stories A).

23

In the garden with Gran

The children love going to stay with Gran. She knows lots of things about nature and wildlife. Gran has lots of fun activities to do in the garden ...

leaf collecting

bark rubbing

making bird feeders

looking at animal tracks

What activities can you do in your garden?

Gran helped Biff, Chip and Nadim to make bird feeders to hang in the garden. Follow the instructions to make your own.

stargazing

You will need:

nuts

a cup

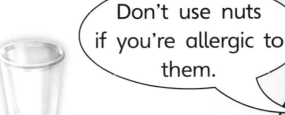

Don't use nuts if you're allergic to them.

seeds

string or wool

lard or fat

What to do:

1. Mix the nuts and seeds in a bowl.

2. Ask an adult to melt the fat and to pour it into the bowl of nuts and seeds. Mix it all together.

3. Ask an adult to help you to make a hole in the bottom of your cup. Thread wool through the hole and tie a knot inside.

4. Pour the mixture into the cup.

5. Let it set.

6. Take the cup off.

7. Hang it up.

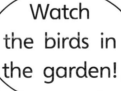

Watch the birds in the garden!

Now read *Homework!* (Level 6 More Stories B).

Telling a story

This is a story map showing a magic key adventure. Each picture shows an important part of the story. Use the pictures and the descriptions to tell the story in your own words.

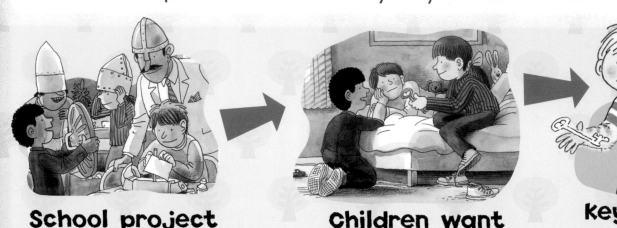

School project on Vikings

Children want key to glow

Key glows

Biff's torch scares raiders

Raiders attack Viking village

Raiders leave

Vikings give Biff a shield

Children taken to a Viking longship

Vikings find them

Land at Viking village

Meet villagers

Key glows

Biff takes the shield to school

Now you can ...

- change part of the story
- think of a new ending
- even make up a new magic key adventure.

 Now read *Viking Adventure* (Level 8 Stories).

Making a Biff, Chip and Kipper book

Roderick Hunt and Alex Brychta work together to make the stories.

Roderick imagines the whole story from beginning to end.

Roderick writes the story.

Roderick works with an editor to check the story through.

Roderick and Alex have a meeting to talk about the story. Alex draws sketches of each page.

Alex draws and colours the artwork for the book.

The artwork and the text of the story are put together to make a book.

From blank page to finished artwork

This is how Alex Brychta draws his artwork.

Later, they saw a shop that sold bodyboards.

Gran spoke to Dad. "Will you let me get one each for the children? It can be my holiday treat."

1. The text for the story is put into the pages as it will look in the book.

Later, they saw a shop that sold bodyboards.

Gran spoke to Dad. "Will you let me get one each for the children? It can be my holiday treat."

2. Alex draws a sketch of the artwork in a meeting with Roderick.

Later, they saw a shop that sold bodyboards.

Gran spoke to Dad. "Will you let me get one each for the children? It can be my holiday treat."

3. Then he draws it all again and adds in lots of detail.

Later, they saw a shop that sold bodyboards.

Gran spoke to Dad. "Will you let me get one each for the children? It can be my holiday treat."

4. Finally, he paints in the colours.

Author and illustrator

Roderick Hunt

Roderick Hunt lives in Oxfordshire in a house very like the house in the magic key adventures. Roderick has been writing stories for many years and he has written over 300 Biff, Chip and Kipper stories so far.

Alex Brychta

Alex Brychta has worked on cartoon films and illustrated books. Alex has drawn Biff, Chip and Kipper stories for many years – he has drawn Floppy about 50 000 times now, but still loves drawing him.

Write your own story

Can you think of a new adventure for Biff, Chip and Kipper?

Step 1.

Start with an idea for your story. Where would you like Biff, Chip and Kipper to go? Who would you like them to meet? You could use a story that you have read and retell it in your own words or you could make up a new adventure for the children.

Step 2.

Plan the details of your story by writing down ideas and key words. Every story has a beginning, a middle and an end.

Beginning

Where does your story start?

Which children will go on the adventure?

How will they get to the magic adventure? Look at pages 16-17 to see how the magic key works.

Middle

Where has the magic taken the children?

Who do they meet?

Who do they help?

What happens? What do they do?

End

Have the children helped someone or solved a problem?

How do they get home again?

Do they bring anything back with them?

Step 3.

It is time to start writing your story. Remember to write in full sentences. Don't forget to think about exciting words you can use, spelling and punctuation.

You could make a book and add pictures to show what is happening in the story.

Step 4.

When you have finished, read your story aloud to a friend.

Story time

If words were threads of wool and silk,
Which weave rich cloths of red and gold,
Then on our classroom wall we'd hang,
The stories Mrs May has told.

"What time is it?" asks Mrs May.
Then quickly we all gather round.
"It's 'Once Upon a Time'," we say,
And sit like mice, without a sound.

"Which story shall we have today?"
Asks Mrs May with twinkling eyes,
"That funny one you've heard before?
Or one that takes you by surprise?"

Ah! We've been places long ago,
In stories Mrs May has told,
Heard tales of mermaids, knights and gnomes,
Of children brave and true and bold.

What tales she weaves! What yarns she spins!
She makes us laugh. She makes us sigh.
We've gasped and cheered. We've shouted no.
Heard one so sad, it made us cry.

If tales were cloths of coloured silk,
Here's something that we know for sure,
Our favourite ones, we'd all take home,
And keep them safe for ever more.

Share this poem with a grown up. Read it aloud to them and talk about the poem together.

Answers

Pages 4–5 *Spot the difference*

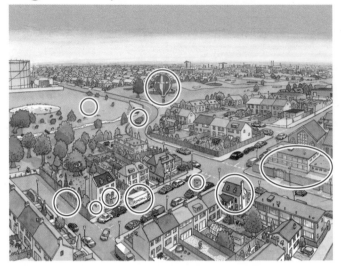

If you want to read the children's favourite adventures, they are:

Biff *The Blue Eye* (Level 9 More Stories A), **Chip** *Save Floppy!* (Level 8 More Stories A), **Kipper** *Robin Hood* (Level 6 Stories), **Wilf** *The Hunt for Gold* (Level 7 More Stories A), **Wilma** *The Quest* (Level 9 Stories), **Anneena** *The Flying Machine* (Level 9 More Stories A), **Nadim** *Storm Castle* (Level 9 More Stories A), **Lee** *The Ogre's Dinner* (Level 8 Decode and Develop)

If you liked this book...

There are hundreds of stories about Biff, Chip and Kipper. You can read some of them as free eBooks on our Oxford Owl website or you can read the books!

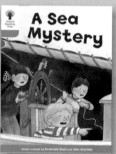

Try reading Biff, Chip and Kipper Companion 1.

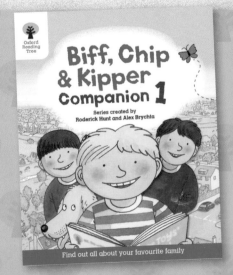